Predictive Analytics

The Secret to Predicting Future Events Using Big Data and Data Science Techniques Such as Data Mining, Predictive Modelling, Statistics, Data Analysis, and Machine Learning

Contents

Introduction

The following chapters will discuss everything that you need to know when it comes to what predictive analysis does and why we all should learn how to use this process when it comes to our raw data. There is an enormous amount of raw data coming to us from all angles, data that businesses are taking in all the time. But the important part here is not how much data they can take in, but how they are able to use this data to learn something new, to find new trends, and to make predictions on how they should behave and act in the future. This guidebook will help you understand one of the processes that you can use - the predictive analysis - that will help when it is time to make some of these predictions.

The beginning of this guidebook explores the basics that come with predictive analysis. We will look at how this works, and why it is so beneficial to use this process. We can then take a look at some of the different methods that you can use during your predictive analysis in order to make these big predictions, including data mining, big data, predictive modeling, statistics, and data analysis.

Next, we'll move on to a few of the other topics that are going to come into play when it is time to work with predictive analysis. We will add in a bit of an introduction to machine learning and how this can help with making predictions, and some of the options that you should follow when you want to avoid the prediction traps, the biases, and more that can interfere with the predictions that you want to make with these processes.

Towards the end of this guidebook, we are going to spend some time looking at the best steps that you can take to make sure that your predictive analysis is as successful as possible. There are a few ways that we can do this, but we will start with some of the top reasons to use predictive analysis in your business and why it is so beneficial, and some of the top steps to help you create one of your own predictive analysis models to help take that raw data and make it as useful as possible in your life.

There are a lot of different methods that you can implement to go through all of the raw data that your company regularly retains. Rather than trying to guess the kind of decisions you should make without any proof or data behind these decisions, why not use predictive analysis to help avoid this risk and improve your business decisions? When you are ready to learn more about predictive analytics and how it can work for your needs, this guidebook will show you how to get started.

Chapter 1: The Basics of Predictive Analysis

The first topic that we need to consider is predictive analysis. This topic will be the common thread that we explore throughout this guidebook. As such, having a good understanding of what this all means and how we can use this to our advantage is going to be so important to how well we can do with some of the other topics in this guidebook as well.

To start with, predictive analysis is helpful when we use data, machine learning techniques, and other statistical algorithms to help us identify the likelihood of an outcome in the future, usually based on some of the data that we have from the past. The goal of using this is to go beyond just knowing what has happened so that we can then come up with a good assessment of what we think will happen in the future.

Of course, this is not always going to be accurate all of the time. Sometimes, the future doesn't behave in the way that we would expect, or some big changes in the economy or the market have delivered results that no one is expecting. But the idea here is that we want to use this kind of analysis because often, the way the company has done in the past is like how they will do in the future, as long as all things remain constant.

This could be used when you are trying to figure out how to schedule employees based on sales, for example. If it is a cold winter, and you had lower sales the last few colder winters, then it is likely that you will not schedule as many people to handle all the shifts because there won't be as much traffic. If you make some big sales around Christmas time, then you would want to make sure you schedule more shifts at the right times to handle this higher business level.

Though the work of predictive analysis is something that we have seen around for decades, it is a technology that is starting to seem more valuable recently. There are a lot of organizations throughout all the different industries which are seeing the value of this kind of analysis, and they are turning to it to see how they can benefit. The point of doing this is because it provides the company with a big advantage over the competition, and it can even help their bottom line. But this brings up the question, why is the idea of predictive analysis becoming so popular now, even though it is something that has been around for quite some time?

There are actually a couple of different reasons for this. Some of these reasons include:

1. There is a growing amount of data types that companies are using and gathering now. In fact, many companies have more data now than they have ever had in the past, and they need to know how to use it. There is also a growing interest in using this data in an efficient way to produce insights that are valuable and can help the business to perform better.
2. Computers that are faster and less expensive.
3. Software that is easier than ever before to use on a variety of tasks.
4. Economic conditions that are tougher, which means that each company - no matter what kind of industry they are in -

needs to be able to differentiate themselves from the competition.

With software that is interactive and easier to use than ever before, and with the fact that this is becoming more prevalent all the time, predictive analytics is no longer just the domain of statisticians and mathematicians, as it was in the past. Line-of-business experts and business analysts are now opening and using a lot of these same technologies for their companies as well.

We can also take a look at why this predictive analytics is going to be so important. Organizations are going to turn to this analytics in order to help them solve some difficult problems, and uncover some new opportunities. This means that there is already a lot of opportunities out there for this kind of process already.

With this in mind, some of the common uses that we are going to see with predictive analysis will include the ability to detect fraud. Because predictive analysis is able to combine together multiple methods of analytics, it is able to improve the detection of patterns and prevent a lot of criminal behavior. As the world is on the lookout for more types and more advancements in the cyberattacks that come, being able to have the right kinds of analytics in place can make sure that all the abnormalities that are present can be caught ahead of time and can keep personal and financial information as safe as possible.

Another benefit is going to come in the form of optimizing the marketing campaigns. Predictive analytics will help companies and marketers determine the purchases or the responses of the customer, as well as help promote some of the cross-selling opportunities as soon as they come up. Predictive models are going to be able to help with this because they are good for assisting a business in attracting, retaining, and growing some of their customers who are the most profitable.

You can also use these predictive models to help with improving operations. Many companies are going to use these predictive models to forecast inventory and manage the resources that they have. For example, this is something that you will see with airline tickets because they will use these models to ensure they set the ticket prices at the right point, based on the demand at that time of year. Hotels can do this by predicting how many guests are going to show up on any given night, maximizing occupancy and increasing their revenue at the same time. When predictive analytics is used properly, it is going to enable the organization to function in a manner that is more efficient, increasing their bottom line.

We can see how predictive analytics can come into play and reduce the amount of risk that the company is going to assume. For example, credit scores are often used because they can do an assessment of how likely it is a buyer will default on their purchases, and it is one of the best-known examples of how this predictive analysis is going to be able to work.

The score that you get on your credit is actually a number that has been generated through the use of predictive analysis, based on some of your past habits with making purchases, asking for and either receiving or being denied for a loan when you apply, whether you have made payments on time in the past and more. Other risk-related uses of this kind of model are going to include things like the claims and the collections that you try to do with your insurance company over time.

With this in mind, we also need to take a look at who is using this kind of model in order to gain a competitive advantage over others in the same industry. Pretty much any industry will be able to use this predictive analysis to help them to increase their revenue, optimize how they run the company, and to reduce the risks that they face. But there are a few industries already jumping on board and seeing a lot of benefits in the process. These industries are going to include:

Banking and Financial Services. The financial industry is often going to handle a huge amount of money and data on a regular basis. In between people putting money into and taking money out of their accounts, the various loans they offer, and more, it is no wonder that this industry is going to use some of the predictive analytic models to help them out. They can use these models to help out with the detection and the reduction of fraud, to help measure the credit risk of various customers, to maximize the cross-sell or the upsell opportunities, and to make sure that they will retain valuable customers along the way.

One example of this is done with the Commonwealth Bank. They have been able to utilize the predictive analysis models in a way that they can figure out the likelihood of fraud pretty quickly. This company can predict how likely it is that fraud is occurring for any given transaction before that transaction has been authorized - *within 40 milliseconds of the initiation* of a particular transaction.

Think of how this can change the financial world. It builds up a lot of trust with the bank because it is more likely they will catch someone who is trying to make fraudulent purchases long before they can get away with anything. It helps to put the mind of the customer at rest because they know their money is safe, and often the check for fraud is done without anyone even noticing because it is that quick. The bank is also going to benefit. They can save billions of dollars in the process if they can stop fraudulent charges before they even happen, saving time doing investigations into the transactions, and the potential for losing the money because the person who did it was never caught will go down to a minimum as well.

Next on the list: Oil, Gas, and Utilities. Whether these companies are predicting when equipment will fail so they can get things fixed or replaced quickly without a bit interruption, or they are predicting the future needs of their resources, mitigating safety and reliability risks, or trying to improve their performance overall, the energy industry has really taken a liking to predictive analytics and using it on a daily basis.

A good example of how this has been used is with the Salt River Project. This is the second largest of the public power utilities in America, and one of the largest suppliers of water in Arizona. Analysis of machine sensor data is able to help this company predict when their turbines, the ones that give power, need some maintenance along the way.

Retail companies can benefit from this kind of analysis, as well. At one point, a study that is now infamous shows that men who go to the store to buy diapers also will purchase some kind of beer at the same time. And since this time, retailers have been using predictive analytics to help them plan out their merchandise and optimize the prices that they sell things to. This allows them to see how effective their promotional events can be, and will make it easier to determine which offers are the best to start.

While many retailers do this on a regular basis, we are going to take a look at Staples for a moment. Staples was able to use predictive analysis to gain customer insight. They analyzed behavior, which gave them a complete picture of their customers. When they were able to put this into practice, it resulted in a return on investment of 137 percent.

We can also see **governments and the public sector** using this kind of technology. Governments have already been one of the key players when it comes to the advancement of computer technologies. For example, the US Census Bureau has been analyzing data to help understand trends in the population for a long time. To add to this, governments now use predictive analytics like many other industries so that they can improve their performance and their service, so they can detect and then prevent fraud, and help them better understand the behavior they see with the consumer. They can often add in cybersecurity to their use of predictive analysis.

The health insurance industry uses predictive analysis as well. This can be a risky business because you want to provide the best service to customers, but you must balance out the costs that it takes to help patients with the amount that you are receiving each month. And predictive analysis can really help to make all this fit together.

First, predictive analysis is going to help when it is time to detect fraudulent claims. This industry is taking it a bit further, though, by taking steps to identify patients who are at most risk of chronic disease and then find out what kinds of interventions are going to be the best to help them out. This can help keep the patient healthier while saving the insurance company a lot of money in the long run.

For example, Scripts, who is a large pharmacy benefits company, has used predictive analysis. They use these analytics in order to identify those who are not adhering to their prescribed treatments, which has helped them to save somewhere between $1500 and $9000 per patient. This can help the insurance company lower costs while still giving their customers the healthcare and medicines that they need.

We can also see some of this predictive analysis show up in the world of manufacturing as well. For these companies, it is important for those running it to identify factors that could lead to reduced quality and even to failures in production. They also need to focus on optimizing the parts, the service resources, and the distribution.

One example of the world of manufacturing using this analysis is with the company Lenovo. This is just one of the manufacturers recently who has started to use these predictive analytics in order to understand more about their warranty claims. This was a big initiative in the company that led to an up to 15 percent reduction in warranty costs, saving a lot of time and money overall for the company.

With this in mind, we need to look at some of the information about how the predictive model is going to work. These models can take known results and use them to develop - or train - a model that can be used to help us predict values for different or new data that shows up. Modeling is going to provide us results in the form of a prediction, which will just be the probability of the target variable, based on the estimated amount of significance from a set of input variables.

This is actually going to be a bit different from what we will see with descriptive models. With the descriptive models, we use them to help us understand what happened. And then there are diagnostic models that are a bit different as well because they will help us to understand some of the key relationships that go on in the business, and then we can use this to determine why something has happened. There are entire books that have been devoted to analytical methods and various techniques, as well. But we will focus on just some of the basics that come with this to help us see how it all works.

The first thing to explore here is the two different types of predictive models that we can work with. The classification models are going to be able to predict class membership. For example, you may want to do a model on whether any of your employees are likely to leave, whether a customer is going to respond to a solicitation, and whether the customer is going to be a bad or good credit risk for you.

Usually, the model is going to give us results that come in the form of 0 (zero) or 1 (one) so that it stays binary and is easier to work with overtime. 1 is going to be the event that you are targeting, and 0 means that the event you are targeting is not going to happen.

Then we can also work with the regression models. These are the models that are able to predict a number for us. This means that they can help us see how much revenue a customer is able to generate over the next year, or the number of months before we think a component is going to fail on one of our machines, so we can make sure to order it and get that part fixed in a timely manner without stopping production.

With this in mind, there are also a few different techniques that you are able to work with when you use predictive modeling. The three most common options are going to include *neural networks, regression, and decision trees*. To start with is the decision tree. These are going to be models of classification that can partition your data into various subsets based on the categories that you use for the variables of input.

This is going to make it easier to understand the path someone took to make their decisions. A decision tree is given this name because it looks like a tree with each branch representing a choice between a number of alternatives, and each leaf representing a classification or a decision. This model can be useful because it will look at the data and then tries to find the one variable that can split that data into groups that are the most different.

Decision trees can be popular because they are easy for us to interpret and understand. They also will help you handle any missing values that show up, and can be useful for preliminary variable selection. So, any time you are working with a set of data and you have a value that is missing, or you would like to work with an answer that is quick and easy to interpret, you can start making a decision tree.

You can also work with *regression* when creating a predictive model. Both logistic and linear work here. This is actually one of the most popular out of the methods in statistics because it is going to help estimate the relationships that are there between variables. It is intended to use with continuous data that we can assume is following a normal distribution, and it can help find key patterns in the larger sets of data. And sometimes, a programmer will use it to determine how much specific factors, including the price, will influence the movement we see with an asset.

When you use the regression analysis, you want to be able to predict a number, and then the response of this is going to be the Y variable. With the linear regression option, one of the independent variables will be used to help explain and predict the outcome you will get with Y. Multiple regression can come in as well and we will use two or more independent variables to predict the outcome.

With logistic regression, though, the unknown variable of a discrete variable is going to be predicted based on known values of the other variables. The response variable is going to be categorical, meaning that it is only able to take on a limited number of values. When we do the binary logistic regression, a response variable only has two values, including 0 or 1. In multiple logistic regression, a response variable can sometimes come with several levels, including 1, 2, and 3, or low, medium, and high

And the third type of model that you can work with is the *neural networks*. These are going to be sophisticated techniques that are capable of modeling relationships that are really complex. These are going to be popular in this kind of field because they are so flexible and so powerful in the process. The power with them is going to come in because they have the ability to handle any of the relationships that show up in the data that are nonlinear, which is going to show up more and more as companies work to gather more data from their customers, and from other sources.

These neural networks are going to be there to help us to confirm the findings that we may see with some of the other techniques, including the decision tree and the regression. They are going to work because they are based on pattern recognition and some of the artificial intelligence processes to model the parameters that you would like graphically.

They are going to work well, even when you do not have a known mathematical formula that will relate to the input or the output, and when the prediction is going to be the most important thing in the mix – even more important than the explanation. You can also work with the neural network when you have a good amount of training data to use in teaching the algorithm or the method the right way to behave.

Knowing a bit of artificial intelligence with this can make things easier because a lot of the methods that work with this idea, including machine learning, can make the neural network stronger. In fact, the artificial neural networks were originally developed by researchers who were trying to mimic the neurophysiology of the human brain.

These are the most common types of techniques that you can work with when it comes to doing predictive analysis, but there are certainly not the only ones that you are able to work with as you do your own predictive modeling. Learning about the different methods that you can use, and some of the times when you would pull each one out can make a big difference in the amount of success you are going to have with these predictions. We will take some time to discuss a few more of these methods, as well as discussing in more detail the ones above as we go through this guidebook.

Chapter 2: How to Predict Future Events with the Help of Big Data

Now that we have some idea of what the predictive analysis is all about, and why it is so important for helping out a business, it is time for us to look at big data. We did talk before about how data is really important in this kind of analysis. Without the data, we have nothing to base our predictions on in the first place. Knowing what is inside the data, and then using it to make decisions and predictions are what predictive analytics is all about. With that in mind, we need to take some time to understand Big Data and why it has become such an important part of many companies.

Big data is not a concept that is hard to understand or going to be complex. It is simply the term that we use in order to describe a large volume of data. Sometimes this data is going to be structured, and other times it is going to be unstructured. This is the data that will come into a business on a day to day business. Some companies have a lot of data, and some are not going to have as much, but the interesting thing here is that the amount of data is not really that important.

What is important, and what we will need to focus on here when we do predictive analysis, is what the company is going to do with the data, big or small, that really matters. Yes, Big Data usually refers to a large amount of data that the company has. But we really need to focus on how that data is handled and used by the company to see what will happen with them.

A company can have all of the data in the world. But if they choose not to use it, just store it away for later, or if they don't understand the data, then it doesn't do them any good at all. They may as well have no data on them at all. This is where the predictive analysis is going to come into play, though. It helps the company to take all of the data they are holding onto, and analyze it for various insights and trends that may be hidden in there, leading to the best decisions and strategic moves for the business.

The term "Bog Data" is a relatively new concept, and it wasn't heard in the world of business until the last few years; we can all agree that companies have been gathering, as well as storing, large amounts of information to analyze at some point for a long time. This is how they come up with their current advertisements, their promotions, their new products, and more - all in order to entice their customers to make a purchase.

It was in the early 2000s when this concept started to gain some momentum. This happened when Doug Laney, one of the analysts in the industry, articulated a now mainstream definition of what big data is all about. Remember, it is not necessarily just about the amount of data that you are holding onto; it is about a few other things as well. The best way to remember what Big Data is about is to remember the "three Vs" which include the following:

1. **Volume.** Organizations are able to collect data from a large variety of sources, which can include information they get from their machine to machine data, from their various social media accounts, and from business transactions. In the past, they may have limited the amount of data they take in

because of the storage, but with some of the newer options available, this is a burden that is a bit easier to handle.

2. **Velocity.** Data is able to stream into a company at speeds that are unprecedented and hard to keep up with. Even though it is a ton of data that is coming in quickly, it still has to be dealt with in a manner that is timely if the company wants to still gain some insights out of it. Smart metering, sensors, and tags are helping many companies to deal with this information in a timely manner, at least as much as possible, so that companies can keep up and gain the right predictions out of that information.

3. **Variety.** We have to remember during this process that variety is going to be important with the data that we use. Data is going to come to our direction from lots of formats. This can include text documents that are not structured, numeric data that is found in a traditional database, and structured data as well. We can also see things like financial transactions, stock ticker data, audio, email, and video, to name a few.

It is the responsibility of the business to be able to handle all these varieties of data and learn the best way to get them to conform with one another to give you results.

We can also take this idea a little bit further. In addition to the "three Vs" that we talked about before, it is also possible for us to use a few other ideas to help understand Big Data and what it is all going to be about. The other two parts of Big Data that are important will include:

1. **Variability.** In addition to the increasing varieties and velocities that happen with the data, the data flow can be inconsistent throughout the month or year. There are going to

be times with higher flow, and times with lower flow. Daily, event-triggered, and seasonal peak data loads can be hard for us to manage sometimes. And this becomes an even bigger problem when we deal with data that is unstructured. Having a plan in place and learning when these peaks can help your business to thrive.

2. **Complexity:** Today's data is going to come from multiple sources, which is going to add in another layer of challenge for us to link, cleanse, match, and transform data across the systems. However, it is important for a company to be able to connect and then correlate relationships, multiple linkages in data, and hierarchies in the data – or that data is going to start spiraling out of control!

This brings us to the next point that we need to consider. We need to take a look at why this Big Data is so important, and why we are taking some time now to discuss it and learn more about it. The importance of this big data is not going to revolve just around how much data you are holding onto, but what you plan to do with that data. You can basically take that data from any source that you would like, and a few things are going to happen.

When you analyze the Big Data, you will find that it can help you get answers that enable a reduction in costs for the company, a reduction in the amount of time that it takes to get things done, the ability to develop some new products, and optimized offerings, and it can increase the number of smart decisions that you can make.

When you can combine this Big Data together with high powered analytics or something like predictive analysis, you are going to be able to accomplish a wide range of business-related tasks. Some of these tasks include:

1. Helping you to determine some of the root causes of failures, defects, and issues in real-time, making it easier to fix the issue and get things back on track.

2. Monitoring the customers you have and then generate coupons at the point of sale. These coupons are going to be based on the buying habits of the customer.

3. Looking at the portfolio that you have and then recalculate the amount of risk that is found there in just a few minutes rather than in hours.

4. It is great at detecting behavior that is more fraudulent before it is going to have any kind of effect on your organization.

Big data is going to have a big effect on all organizations, no matter which industry you are looking at. In fact, all of the industries that we talked about before when it comes to the predictive analysis are also going to benefit from the use of Big Data. Plus, there are many others who are on board and seeing the benefits as well. Let's take a moment to look at the industries that use Big data on a regular basis now, and how they are able to benefit from all of this new information coming in.

First on the list is banking. Just think about the number of transactions that banks and other financial institutions have to deal with on a regular basis. They have to keep track of debit and credit card purchases, people depositing money into their accounts, loan information, and more. And they have to make sure that no fraudulent activity is going to happen in the meantime. This can make it hard to keep up and to make sure that the money is safe and sound throughout the day.

Big Data is going to come in because it helps with all of this. This brings in a lot of big insights on the customers that the business has, while also requiring that the financial institutions always stay a step ahead of the game when it comes to advanced analytics. The bank or financial institution will be able to use the Big Data to help them to pick out the right individuals to give loans to, to watch for activity that may be criminal in the purchases, and more, saving them a lot of money.

Education can use this Big Data as well. Educators, when they are armed with insights that are driven by all of that data, are able to make a huge impact on the school system, the curriculum that they work with, and their own students. This Big Data is also going to come into play when they can analyze it and then identify students who may be more at risk than others.

With this information in hand, the teacher and others at the school are able to find the students who need the most help, watch to make sure that they are making good progress, and even come up with a better system of support and evaluation for principals and teachers to ensure that everyone is on the same page the whole time.

Another industry that is going to benefit from all of this Big Data is health care. Think about how much information goes through a hospital or a clinic. Many times a patient is going to have at least a few records just for going in for their regular checkups. Then if they ever have surgery, give birth, have to get a scan done, get referred out to a specialist, change insurance, or anything else, this is more information that the hospital or the clinic is going to need to take care of as well.

Between prescription information, plans on treatment, and patient records, everything has to be done in a quick and accurate manner in this kind of industry. There also has to be enough transparency that goes on to satisfy all of those stringent regulations in the industry. When this data is handled in the right manner, the providers can do their job better, and can even uncover some of the insights that are hidden in all of that information, improving the care for the patient.

The world of retail is another place where we can use this big data as well. Customer relationship is going to be so important when it comes to the world of retail, and the best way to make sure that the company can improve that relationship is for them to manage big data and find the insights that are hidden inside.

Retailers have to know the best way that they can market to their customers, the most effective ways that they are able to handle the transactions, and even the most strategic methods they can use when it is time to bring back any business that has lapsed over time. And at the very heart of all of these things, we are going to find Big Data.

Before we move on here, we need to take a look at how big data is going to work. Before we can really see all of the ways that your business is able to benefit from big data at work, we first need to have a better idea of where this data is coming from in the first place. The sources of our big data can come from a lot of different sources, based on what information you are trying to collect. However, the sources that most companies and industries are going to use when bringing in the big data can fall under one of three categories, and these categories to include:

> 1. **Streaming data:** When we look at this category, it is going to include any of the data that is able to reach to your IT system from a web of connected devices. You are able to take a look at and analyze this data as it arrives, and it will make decisions on what data you would like to keep, what you don't want to keep, and what may need you to analyze it a bit further than before.

> 2. **Data from social media:** The data on social interactions is a part that is starting to look even more attractive to many companies, especially when it comes to support, sales, and marketing functions. This kind of data is going to come in the semi-structured or unstructured forms, so it is going to pose a new challenge when you want to use the data or analyze it at all, but it is still useful when you know how to make it show you some good insights.

> 3. **Sources that are publicly available:** There is a massive amount of data that is available to companies through open

data sources - looking for the ones that are available in your industry (and with topics that you are the most interested in) can help you to really see some good information.

After you have had a chance to identify all of the different sources of data that you would like to use, it is now time for you to consider the decisions that you want to make after you harness in all of this information. These do not have to be complicated, but it is still important to have a plan for any and all of the big data that you plan to gather and use for your needs. Some of the decisions that you have to consider and make when it comes to the Big Data you are using will include:

1. *How you would like to store and manage the data.* A few years ago, the storage of all this data was a big issue that companies did not know how to handle. The good news is that there are a lot of low-cost options to hold onto that data now. If this is what you would like to do with the data, then you need to take some time to research and figure out which storage is right for you.

2. *How much of the data you would like to analyze.* This is going to be different for each company based on what they are hoping to get out of the information and what they plan to do as their strategy. Some organizations decide to not exclude any data out of their analysis. This is something that you can do thanks to the high-performance technologies that are out there, such as in-memory analytics or grid computing. But for some companies, it is not necessary to look through all of the data, or it may be too expensive to do this. So, they decide to look at the information and decide which part is relevant, and which part is not before starting the analysis.

3. *How to use the insights that you uncover.* The more knowledge that you have present, the more confident you will be when you make these important business decisions. It is really smart for you to have a strategy in place after you have been able to gather an abundance of information to use.

The final thing that we need to do when it is time to take our Big Data and put it to work for our business is to do some research. This research needs to be done on the various technologies that are available and will help you to make the most out of your big data and can be helpful for your predictive analysis and your big data analytics. Some of the things that you need to consider when you go through this part of the process include:

1. Most of the storage that you can use is cheap, but make sure there is enough room for what you would like to do.

2. You want to work with processors that are faster so it can keep up with this information.

3. You want to go with technologies that are affordable and fit in your budget, open-sourced, and are going to be distributed with the help of big data platforms.

4. You want to consider something like clustering, virtualization, and parallel processing based on how much data you have and what your end goal with all that data is.

5. Many companies also like to work with cloud computing or some other kind of resource that is flexible and allows for arrangements of allocation. It is going to depend on what your end goals are with the data when it comes to which one you would like to use.

The neat thing that comes with big data is that you are able to use it to make the predictions that you want about the future. There is so much information that you are gathering with this Big Data, and the whole point of it is to use this information to learn something about your customers, about your business, and even about your competition and the industry that you are in. If you can use this data in the proper manner, you will find that it is easier to make predictions about what is going to happen in the future.

In fact, many companies are already using this Big Data in order to help them learn insights about their business, and then to make predictions on how things are going to happen in the future. Think of it this way; would you rather just make random decisions and shoot in the dark, hoping that you are going to make the right predictions, or would you rather have a large source of data behind you that points in you in the right direction for the decisions and predictions you make? If you are going with the second choice, then this is exactly where Big Data is going to come in and make a difference. As long as it is used properly, and you have done the right predictive analysis on it, you will find that making predictions with the help of Big Data can be easy.

Chapter 3: Can I Predict Future Events with Data Mining?

Another process that we need to explore a little bit while we are here is the idea of data mining. This is a very important piece of the puzzle when we talk about predictive analysis, and it is going to be so helpful when it is time to make some predictions about whether an event is going to happen with your customers, with your industry, or with your business in the future. Gaining a better understanding of what data mining is all about, and why it is so important can be the key to ensuring you complete your predictive analysis in the proper manner in this process.

To start, we need to take a closer look at what data mining is all about and why it is so important. Data mining is going to be the process of finding anomalies, correlations, and correlations within a large set of data in order to predict the outcomes that are the most likely to happen. There are many techniques that will come into play here, and when you use them properly, it is possible to increase your profits, cut out on costs, improve the relationship that you have with your customers, lower the amount of risk that you are taking on, and so much more as well.

The process of going through all of the data that you have in order to discover some of the hidden insights - then using these insights in order to predict some of the future trends - has been a process that companies have done for many years. In fact, it has been researched quite a bit to see whether this method is effective or not, and it is going to include three intertwined disciplines of science, including machine learning, artificial intelligence, and statistics.

What do all of these mean? Statistics is going to be the numeric study that we can do in order to see what relationship is there in the data. Then we have artificial intelligence, which is when we see what is like human intelligence, displayed by the machines or the software that we use in data mining. And then, machine learning, which is includes all the models and algorithms that we need in order to help look through the data and make predictions. All of these come together to help us through the process of data mining and making predictions based on the information we collect.

Over the last few years, we have also seen that our systems and machines have had some big advances in processing power and speed, and this has allowed us to move beyond some of the time-consuming, tedious, and manual processes that we did in the past. And in its place, we are now onto a data analysis that is automated, quick, and easy, which makes things better for everyone who is involved.

An important thing to note: the more complex the set of data that you can collect, the more potential that you must uncover insights that are relevant and helpful. Yes, it may take longer to get through all of this data, but it means that you are going to find some more insights that can really propel your business forward, and give you a competitive edge over others in the same industry. With more data, it is easier to know what promotions to do, how to reach your customers, the demographics of your customers, and more.

So, why is this process of data mining so important? If you have been in business for any length of time, it is likely you have already seen the numbers, and you know the fact that the volume of data that is produced is doubling every two years. Unstructured data - on its own - can make up at least 90 percent of what we see in the digital universe. But we always have to remember that more information is not going to be the same thing as more knowledge.

When you work with data mining, it is going to allow you to do a few important things. These are going to include:

1. Data mining can make it easier to sift through all the noise, both the chaotic and the repetitive, that is found in any set of data that you want to work with.

2. Data mining is going to help you understand what is relevant, and then it can make good use of that information by assessing it and making predictions based on that information.

3. It can speed up the amount of time that it takes to make informed decisions - decisions that are based on sound data and information.

From here, we need to be able to look at how this data mining is going to work for us. When we look at data mining as a composite discipline, it represents a variety of methods (and techniques) that can be used with a variety of analytic capabilities. And these are all going to come together to address a gamut of organizational needs, ask the right questions, and use varying levels of input or rules from the programmers who design them in order to help us arrive at a good decision.

There are two types of modeling that we can work with here when we do data mining. These will include descriptive modeling and prescriptive modeling, and each one is going to work in a slightly different way to help us get the results that we would like.

First, let's look at what descriptive modeling means in data mining. This uncovers some of the shared similarities that are found in our historical data in the hopes that we can determine the reasons behind failure or success that happened in your business. This could be something as categorizing your customers by their sentiment or their product preferences. There are a variety of techniques that you are able to use to make this work, and some of them are going to include:

1. **Clustering:** This is when you can group together records that are pretty similar.

2. **Anomaly detection:** This is where we are going to identify some of the outliers and whether they are important or if they can tell you something new.

3. **Association rule learning:** This is when we look at our records and see if there are any relationships that show up between all of them or not.

4. **Principal component analysis:** This is the one we will use when we want to take our variables and determine if there is some kind of relationship that shows up there.

5. **Affinity grouping:** This one is going to be used when we want to group people with common interests, or with goals that are similar. This would be something like people who buy X are often going to buy Y at the same time, and they may also purchase Z at the same time.

Another method that we can work with is known as *predictive modeling*. This one is going to be useful because it is able to go deeper in order to help us classify some events in the future or to help us estimate an outcome that is unknown. This could include something like using credit scoring in order to determine how likely it is that an individual will be able to repay one of their loans or not.

Predictive modeling is going to come into play because it can help us to uncover insights for things like the churn of the customer, the credit defaults, and the response of a certain campaign that you did. Some of the examples of techniques that we can use that fit under the umbrella of predictive modeling will include the following:

1. *Regression:* This one is going to be the measure of the strength of a relationship between one dependent variable, and a series of variables that are independent.

2. *Neural networks:* This is when we will use programs on our computers in order to detect the patterns that are found in a set of data, make predictions based on that data as well, and to help us learn from all of that data.

3. *Decision trees:* These will be diagrams shaped like trees where each of the branches represent a probable occurrence that could happen at some point.

4. *Support vector machines:* This is going to be an example of a supervised machine learning algorithm that is going to be able to help us learn more about the data we have

The third type of modeling that we can work with is known as *prescriptive modeling.* With the growth of all the data that is unstructured from the web, books, comment fields, audio, PDFs, and email, along with some of the other sources of text, the adoption of a field that is known as text mining is growing quite a bit. It is related to data mining, and it helps us to gain the ability that we need in order to parse successfully, filter, and transform all of the data that is unstructured to help us work with the predictive model to improve the accuracy of any predictions that we make.

In the end of this process, you do not want to look at data mining as a separate or a standalone kind of entity because pre-processing, which is data exploration and data preparation, and post-processing, which will be things like model performance monitoring, scoring, and model validation, and both are going to be just as important as one another.

Prescriptive modeling looks at both the external and the internal variables and constraints in order to recommend one or more courses of action that you could take. For example, it could be used in a way to help your company decide the best marketing offer to send out to each customer, making this more customizable and easier to work with and increasing the likelihood that you are going to get a sale. Some of the techniques that you are going to be able to use that go along with prescriptive modeling include:

1. **Predictive analytics plus rules:** This is when you will spend some time developing if and then rules from patterns and predicting the outcomes that you want.

2. **Marketing optimization:** This is when we will simulate the most advantageous media mix in real-time in order to increase the amount of return on investment that you are able to get out of every action that you decide to take.

Data mining is going to be such an important thing that you can do when it comes to your predictive analysis. It will ensure that you are able to get ahold of the information that you want and then go through it and mine through it until you find the information that is the most important.

As a company in the modern world, it is likely that you are taking in a ton of information all of the time. And while this is definitely a good thing for your business, it is more about how you use this data, rather than the exact amount or type of data you decide to collect. You can spend all day collecting that data and store it for years to come, but if you don't go through and mine some of that data, and learn the insights that are inside of it, then the data is going to be worthless to you.

Data mining is going to help you to actually get some use out of the data you are working with. Instead of just storing that data on a server or on the cloud, without any idea of what is in it or how you can use it, you can work with data mining in order to get the most out of the data that you collect this can bring you a lot of the important insights and trends that are found in the data, so that you can then, at a later time, go through and complete your predictive analysis. When it comes to getting something out of your data, and making sure that your predictive analysis is going to be successful so you can make good predictions, make sure that you complete a good data mining process on the data ahead of time as well.

Chapter 4: Predicting Future Events with Predictive Modeling

Now that we have had some time to look at data mining and data analytics when it comes to predictive analysis, it is time to move on, taking a look at what is known as predictive modeling. This is slightly different from some of the other topics that we have spent our time on so far, but now it is time to focus on this a bit more and see how it can factor into the predictive analysis that we want to work with.

First, predictive modeling is going to be the process that we are able to use the results that we already know in order to create, process, and then validate a model that we are able to use to forecast future outcomes. It is a tool that we will see in predictive analytics, and it is also part of data mining that helps us to answer the question, "What might possibly happen in the future?"

The whole point of working with predictive modeling and predictive analysis is that we want to be able to look through data and trends and find out what is going to happen next, and the modeling that we are able to do here will help us to get it all done. You must use the right algorithms and the right methods like what we talked about before, but it can help us to make accurate predictions on what is going to happen in the future.

Understanding How Predictive Modeling Works

The rapid migration and change in our world over to digital products has created a sea of data, one that is easily available and accessible to any business who wants to take the time to collect it. Big data is already being utilized by many companies in order to improve the kind of dynamic that is there in the customer to business relationship. This vast amount of data that is collected in real-time, rather than after the fact, is gotten from a variety of sources like cloud computing platforms, cell phone data, internet browsing history, and social media, to name a few.

When we take some time to analyze events that are historical, there is a higher probability that a business is able to predict what would happen in the future, and then they can plan accordingly. Having a machine and some algorithms and models do the work can make this a lot easier. The algorithm can go through the information in no time at all and will ensure that you will see some results and some predictions in no time.

Yes, it is possible for a human to go through this data rather than using the programming and algorithms. But when you have millions of data points, and more data is added all the time, this becomes a huge undertaking that your employees have to handle, and this is not a good thing at all. It is too big of a task - things are going to get missed - and your employees will not be able to keep up with the work or the information that is streaming in on them. This is why it is best to work with the programming and other options that are available to you.

The data that is coming into the company will often be unstructured and really complex, often too complex for humans to be able to get through and analyze in a short amount of time. Because of all the complexity that enormous amounts of data are going to present, companies are going to turn more towards predictive analytics tools to help them make predictions and to forecast the outcome of an event likely to happen in the near future, and then they can make their plans according to this likelihood.

How does this kind of analysis really work?

Now that we know a bit more about the modeling that comes here, we also need to look at how the predictive analysis - the main topic that we are talking about in this guidebook - is going to work. The predictive analytics will help us collect and then process this data in huge amounts while using powerful computers to help us to assess what has happened in the past. When this part of it is done, it is then able to provide us with a good assessment of what it thinks is going to happen in the future.

The predictive analytics can use predictors, or sometimes known features, in order to create predictive models that we can then use to obtain an output. This model is going to help us learn how these different points of data are going to connect with one another. Two of the most widely uses of predictive modeling techniques include the neural networks and the regression that we talked about before.

Other Things to Consider

There are also a few other topics that we should discuss when it comes to working on a predictive model. In the field of statistics, we will look at regression and see that it talks about the linear relationship between the input and the output variables that we would like to use. So, if a predictive model has a linear function, it is going to require one predictor, or one feature, to help us predict what the outcome, or the output, will be in the end.

A good example of this can be seen in the banking industry. In this example, a bank that hopes to detect when fraud or money laundering is about to happen, in the early stages before things start to get really bad, may incorporate a linear predictive model to help them with this. The reason for this is because the main goal of the bank is to know which of its customers are likely to engage in the activities that come with money laundering at one point or another.

To help make this kind of model and ensure that it is accurate, all of the data for the customers of the bank will be presented to the model. Then, the predictive model is going to be built around the dollar value of transfers that each customer was making during the time the bank specified in the model.

During this time, the model is going through a process of learning so that it can easily recognize the difference between the transactions that are normal, and the transactions that are going to include money laundering. The optimal outcome that we get out of this model should be a pattern that will signal when this money laundering is happening, and when it didn't. If the model perceives that there is a pattern of fraud emerging in one customer based on the learning they did, it is going to create a signal for action, and then the fraud analysts at the bank will take over and look into it more closely.

The predictive models are also going to be used with neural networks powered by deep learning and machine learning, which are both going to be fields found in artificial intelligence. The neural networks will be inspired by the way that the brain works, and they are simply created with a web of interconnected nodes in hierarchical levels, which are the basic foundation that we find in artificial intelligence.

One of the most important capabilities of neural networks is their ability to handle a non-linear data relationship better than any other available algorithm. These neural networks can create relationships and patterns between the variables that would be either too time consuming, or impossible, for a human analyst to handle.

So, while a bank is able to go through this model and input some of the known variables, such as the value of transfers initiated by their customers into the model to get the desired outcome of who is the most likely to engage in the laundering of money, a neural network is able to create a pattern and relationships between the input variables, like the geographic location of the user, the time logged in, the IP address, the sender and the recipient of the funds, and other features that could be included when it comes to activities of money laundering.

Some of the other techniques that are used in predictive modeling and that financial institutions like to use, including decision trees, time series data mining, and even the Bayesian analysis. Companies that are going to take advantage of big data through predictive modeling measures are better able to understand how their customers engage with their products and can identify any of the potential opportunities and risks for the company, saving them a lot of time and money in the process.

Working with a predictive model can really help you out a lot here because it ensures that you are able to take all of that big data that you have been collecting, and turn it into something that can make predictions easily for you. And this is one of the biggest goals that comes with predictive analysis. You want to be able to use the information to drive your business decisions, rather than just guessing and hoping your predictions are right. If you are able to use this kind of prediction in the proper manner, you will find that it is easier than ever to know exactly what is going to happen in the future, based off your historical data, and make decisions that can help you beat out the competition. You will see some great results in no time!

Chapter 5: Using Statistics to Help Predict Future Events

We have spent a bit of time bringing up the idea of statistics a few times throughout this guidebook, but we have not gone into much depth about what this means, how this can work, and why we would want to use statistics to help us out with some of these future events. It may seem like math is not something that we need to bring to the table when we are working here, but it can definitely take us where we want to be and can be the step that is needed to help us make accurate predictions that will propel our business forward.

Before we start with this, we need to take a look at a famous statistician and forecaster, Nat Silver, who has been able to make his own name in the industry by predicting the kind of performance that we are able to see with baseball players. He then went on to start his own blog known as FiveThirtyEight, which is known for very accurate predictions in many of the recent political contests out there.

While this may seem like it is beside the point, it is actually going to help us see how statistics can come into play and maybe the answer that we need in order to why we need to use this field to make predictions in the future. In fact, Silver spends some time talking about a few strategies that we are able to focus on to help us know where we are, and what course we want to take, whether we are talking about our own personal future or the future of our business against the competition.

There are a few issues that we are able to pay attention to that can help us to really see a difference in how well we can predict the future, and these will include:

1. Focus more on what is important. There are two great inventions out there, the internet and the printing press, that have helped us to see an increase in the amount of information that is available to us at a fast rate. But just like with Big Data, we do not want to look at all of the information. Some of it may seem like noise, or it may be silly or false. The challenge here is for a business to use statistics to help them focus on the information that actually matters while leaving all the rest behind.

2. There are a lot of issues, and many of them will end up clouding our vision. It is common for people to attach a lot of importance to recent events and the newest data in the set because they seem more dramatic than the others, but most of them are not that important. We also focus on the familiar, so it is likely that a business may stray towards staying where they are, rather than moving forward and making changes that will help them.

3. The best thing that you can do to break out of this kind of tunnel vision and then test your views from the real world, acknowledging some of the mistakes that you may have made in the real world, and the things that you are struggling to let go of now, learn from them and then actually follow the

information that is out there that is meant to help you see some success.

4. Know what a forecast and a prediction are all about. To start, the prediction is going to be a statement that is specific about when and how something is going to occur. A forecast, on the other hand, is a probabilistic statement. Science is not going to be able to predict with 100 percent accuracy when or where an earthquake will occur. But it will be able to forecast with some confidence that in the next 100 years there is going to be a big earthquake that happens in California.

In a similar manner, you can also make these predictions about your own company. You can figure out what is likely to happen over a period of time, rather than the exact date and time, to help you know the right course of action to take.

With some of these in mind, we need to take some time to look at statistics and what it is all about. Why would we want to know more about statistics and all that comes with it, rather than just using some of the other methods that we have been able to look at through this guidebook? Let's see more about this field and where it comes in when we work on our own predictive analysis along the way.

Statistics is going to be one of the forms of mathematical analysis that you can use, one that is able to use a quantified model, representation, and synopses for a given set of experimental data, and sometimes for studies that are done in real life. Statistics studies the methodologies used to gather, review, analyze, and draw the right conclusions from the data that you have. The good news is that there are a number of measures that you are able to use to make this happen, and these options are going to include:

- The mean

- A regression analysis

- Skewness

- Analysis of variance

- Variance

- Kurtosis

We need to take some time to understand statistics a little bit more. Statistics is going to be a term that is used in order to summarize a process that the analyst is going to use to characterize their set of data. If the set of data you have is going to depend on a sample of a larger population for example, then it is possible for the analyst to develop interpretations about the population, and this is going to be based mostly on the statistical outcomes that you get from that particular sample you did the work on.

When you do an analysis using these kinds of techniques, it is going to involve the process of both gathering and evaluating all of the data that you need, and then you have to perform a summary of the data, but it must be done in a format that is more mathematical.

While the word may make some of us a bit nervous about working with, statistics is used in a lot of different disciplines on a regular basis, and it is not that unusual to find it in places like manufacturing, government, humanities, social sciences, physical sciences, business, and psychology to name a few. The data that is statistical is going to be gathered using a sample procedure in most cases, but it can also use other methods on occasion.

There are many options when working with some of the statistical methods, but the two types that are the most common when it comes to analyzing the data that you have will include the inferential statistics and the descriptive statistics. Descriptive statistics are going to be used to help synopsize data from a sample exercising the mean, or sometimes the standard deviation. Or the other hand, the inferential statistics method is going to be used when you have the data, and it is viewed as a type of subclass that goes with the specific population that you are working with.

Different Types of Statistics

Statistics is a general term that is pretty broad, which means that there are going to be a lot of other models that can fit with it. This is perfect, though, because it allows us to see a lot of different ways that we can predict the future with the use of this term. Some of the different types of statistics that you are able to work with will include:

The mean. This is simply the mathematical average of a group of numerals, which needs to include at least two numbers or more. The mean for a set of numbers that you are specifying can be computed in many ways, including the arithmetic mean, which shows how well a specific commodity performs over a specified period of time. Then you have a geometric mean, which shows that the performance results of an investor's portfolio invested in that the same commodity over the same period of time.

The next option is regression analysis. This one can determine the extent to which factors you determine (such as the price of your product or the interest rates) are going to influence the fluctuations of the price of the asset. This is shown in the form of a line that is straight and is usually called linear regression.

You can work with a process that is known as the skewness, as well. This one is a term that you may not have heard about much, but it is still an important part that comes in here. Most sets of data, including the commodity returns and the stock prices, are going to either have a skew that is positive, which means that the curve is skewed a bit towards the left of the average of the data or a negative skew that goes the other way.

We can also focus on working with the process of kurtosis. This kurtosis is going to measure whether the data is going to be light-tailed, which means it is less prone to the outliers - or heavy-tailed - which means that it is more prone to the outliers compared to what we will see when we look at the normal distribution.

The sets of data that are high in the kurtosis are going to come with heavy tails, or lots of outliers, which implies that there is a greater risk with the investment in the form of wild returns that happen on occasion. You have to decide what kind of risk you are willing to take with this one before jumping in to see if it is the right option for you.

It is also possible for the kurtosis to go the other way. This is when the set of data has a kurtosis with a light tail, or there is a lack of lots of outliers. This kind of risk for investors is going to be lower than the others, which can keep the investments safer, by may not give you the same returns that you were able to get with the other option.

Finally, we need to look at what is known as a *variance*. This variance is going to be the measurement of the span of numbers in the set of data. This variance is going to measure out the distance each number in the set is from the mean. Variance can help us out because it allows the investor to determine the amount of risk that they are going to be taking on willingly when they work on a new investment.

As a business, it is important to be able to manage the risk and the reward ratio that you will get when you complete any kind of task or investment. If the risk is higher than the potential reward, it makes sense that you would want to stay away from it because it is more likely that you will lose money, and the amount that you gain is not going to be worth it.

But what happens with those ratios that are in between? There are a lot of areas below the high risk and low reward and figuring out which one is the best for you to take is going to be one of the many challenges that you face as a business owner. Working with statistics is going to be one of the best ways to take a look at this risk to reward ratio that you have, and then can lead you to make the best decisions for your business, whatever this may be in the process. Adding in the right algorithms, and the right kind of statistics to the mix can make this a lot easier to work with.

Using a combination of the methods above, based on what information you are working with - and what you are hoping to get out of that data - can make a world of difference. You will be able to sort through the data that you have and come up with a good idea of what will work and what can help you out the most in the process.

Working with statistics is so important when it comes to a lot of the things that you do with predictive analysis. It can help us to get some of the mathematical parts that we need with the analysis and can ensure that we get the information that we need in the process, making life easier overall. Most of the time, the algorithms that you are going to focus on when doing predictive analysis will use some form of statistics with it, so knowing how this process works can be critical to helping you make some good predictions.

Chapter 6: Bringing Data Analysis Into the Mix to Make Predictions

Another part of the puzzle that we need to bring out here is the idea of data analysis. Just like with some of the other elements that we have spent some time discussing in this guidebook, the data analysis is going to be essential and can help us make some predictions on the data that we bring in. This method may seem similar to some of what we have been able to talk about so far in this guidebook, but it is going to take a slightly different approach, and it is still a good idea for us to take a look at this and see how it can come into the mix to make some reasonable predictions.

To start, we need to take a look at what this data analysis is all about. Data analysis is going to be the practice where we can take some of the raw data that we have and then order and organize it in such a way that it becomes useful, allowing us to cull the important insights and trends that we need from it. It recognizes that with all of this data, there is going to be some good information, but there will also be a lot of noise and a lot of outliers that we need to be careful about, and that we can probably ignore without missing out on too much in the process.

The process of organizing and then thinking about the data that we have is going to be a big key to understanding what the data has inside and what it is not holding onto. There are a lot of ways that someone can come and approach what they see with data analysis, and it is notoriously easy to manipulate the data to say and behave the way that you want during the analysis phase. This allows some people to push the agendas and the conclusions that they want, rather than actually looking at the facts that are presented.

This is why we need to be really careful with the data and that we don't try to manipulate it at all. There is a lot of good insights that are found in the data that we want to look through, but if we start to mess around with the data and not treat it the way that we should, then we are going to make bad decisions that we think are driven by the data, but really are not, and this can harm our business as a whole.

Because of the ability to manipulate and read the data wrong, it is important always to be critical when we look at the information that we are presented. It is important also to pay attention when we have someone presenting data analysis to us and to think critically about any of the data that we see, and the conclusions that the other person was able to draw.

You may also find, as we have discussed before, that the raw data that we will use in this kind of analysis can come in many forms. This could include any observations that the company took, the responses to surveys that were sent out, and even some measurements. The one that you use, and it is possible to work with more than one if needed, is going to depend on the kind of data that you are trying to work with, and some of your overall goals when you start collecting the data in the first place.

When you have the data in the raw form, you have a ton of data, and often the information is going to be really overwhelming, even if it is really useful for your business. Over the course of the process that you do with data analysis, you will be able to order the raw data in a way that can turn it into something that makes no sense into something that is a lot more useful.

For example, when you first get in the surveys that you send out to your customers, this is going to seem like an extraordinary amount of information that you need to keep track of, and you may feel like you will never get through it to see the insights. But as you go through and tally up the information that you have, you can start to make charts and graphs that can help you see, just at a glance, who answered the survey and what results they were able to give to you along the way.

During your time organizing all of this data, it is likely that you are going to see a variety of trends emerge in the process. These trends are important because you can highlight them in the write up of the data, ensuring that your readers notice the same thing that you do and that they will take this kind of thing into consideration.

Let's say that you were doing a kind of causal survey of preferences when it comes to the type of ice cream someone likes. In this survey, after you went through and asked a big group of people and tallied the information, you found that more women compared to men had a fondness for chocolate. Depending on what your goals are with this kind of survey, this point may be of interest to the person conducting the survey. Being able to model the data with the help of many tools, including mathematics, can sometimes help us to exaggerate these points of interest that show up in the data, which is always going to make it easier for the researcher to see.

There are a lot of different points that are going to show up in the data analysis that you do. Some examples of these are going to include a textual writeup, graphs, and charts. These methods were designed in order to refine and then distill the data so that the readers were able to get some of the interesting information from all of that data, without having to take all of that large set of data and sort through it on their own.

You will find during this process that summarizing the data is going to be so critical to the supporting arguments and can ensure that you can maintain some of the arguments that you have as well. It also helps us when we want to present the data in a manner that is understandable and clear. This makes it easier for those who are responsible for hearing about the information to know what is inside and can make it helpful when it is time to make some important decisions based on that information.

There are a variety of methods that you are able to use in order to help summarize the data and make sure that the person who needs to see it will be able to understand what is there. Using the charts and graphs are often the best option here, but many times a data scientist is going to add in the raw data that they have in an appendix so that others are able to look up the specifics and double-check the work that they did to build more trust in the process.

When many data scientists encounter the data and the conclusions that are summarized, it is likely that they are going to take them at face value. This is not always the best idea, though, because it is important to know how these conclusions were formed, and whether it is actually something that is accurate or not

Everyone who sees this data needs to be able to take a look at it in a critical manner. Asking where the data is from can be really important, as is asking about the method that was used for sampling to collect the data, and the size of the sample that was used in the process. It is the source of the data that appears to have a conflict of interest with the type of data that you are being gathered, and this can call the results into question if you are not happy with the conflict of interest that is there.

Researchers who are reputable and trying to actually come up with good and accurate results will make sure that these conflict of interests are not present and will be able to provide the information about all of their data gathering techniques that are used, the source of the funding that helped them to get the work done, and the point of why they collected the data in the beginning so that those who are looking at the data are able to think through whether this is a source of the data that you would like to use.

The good news is that many of the options you use for the data analysis that are used, such as government sources and many of the independent options, are going to be good to work with, and you won't run into this issue. But it is always a good idea to go through and double-check the sources of all the data you are looking for to make sure there isn't a conflict of interest, and to make sure that the data actually supports the conclusions that you are seeing. This will ensure that the data you are using, no matter what you are using it for, will actually be useful for what you would like.

Data analysis is going to be an important section when we work on this process. It is going to ensure that we will see some good results in the process, and makes it easier for us to really take the raw data that we have, and put it into a form that is the most useful to us. Learning how to analyze the data that you have after it is gathered, and even working with some charts and other visualizations can be so important to get the most out of this type of analysis while making some good predictions for your company based on the data.

Chapter 7: Using Machine Learning to Make the Predictions For You

The next topic that we need to spend some time learning about is known as machine learning. Machine learning is a great process to work with because it can take a lot of the analysis that we have already talked about in this guidebook, and will provide the actual power that helps us come up with the predictions that we use in our decision making. You will find that without these algorithms, you may have to go through manually and look through all of this data, and that is wasteful and time-consuming. And with machine learning, there are a lot of choices in the algorithms that you want to use, which can make your life easier to handle any kind of data that you would like.

Before we dive into how machine learning can be used to make predictions, we first need to take a look at what machine learning is all about. Machine learning is going to be a technique that you can use in data analytics that will teach the computer to do what seems to come pretty naturally to animals and humans. What we mean by this is that we can use various techniques to teach a computer how to learn from past experiences.

How does this work? Machine learning works with algorithms that will use a variety of computational methods to learn information directly from data without relying on an equation that is predetermined as a model. The algorithm can adaptively learn how to improve their performance as the number of samples available for learning increases.

For example, your data set could be limited in the beginning because you don't have as much information available. You still use that to do the training and the testing to get the algorithm up and running. After that time, as you add in more data, and the algorithm can learn along the way, you will find that the algorithm gets stronger and will be able to make more accurate predictions as well.

Machine learning is going to be a method of data analysis that is able to automate the process of building analytical models. It is also a branch of artificial intelligence that is going to be based on the whole idea that a system is able to learn from the data it is presented, it can identify the patterns that are there, and it is even able to make its own decisions without a lot of intervention from humans in the process.

Because of all the new computing technologies that are out there, machine learning - as we know it today - is not really the same as the machine learning that we see in the past. It was born out of a form recognition for patterns and the idea of how a computer is able to actually learn, without a programmer there, to ensure it performs a task specifically. Researchers who were interested in some of the things that we are able to do with artificial intelligence also wanted to see if their machines were able to learn from data that it was fed.

The iterative aspect that comes with this machine learning should be seen as an important programming tool because as we expose any of the models we create from this learning to new data, the model is then able to adapt on their own and independently. The machine is going to be able to learn what has happened to it in the past, and the examples it was given, in order to make accurate and reliable predictions in the future.

Thanks to the rise that we see with big data, machine learning is starting to become one of the big techniques that are there to help with a lot of different areas of solving problems. Some of the biggest areas that are going to be able to use machine learning to help solve their problems will include:

1. Computational finance This is when the financial world can use machine learning to help with things like algorithmic trading and credit scoring, to name a few processes.

2. Computer vision and image processing. This is when we can use machine learning to help with processes like object detection, motion detection, and facial recognition.

3. Computational biology. This is when we will use machine learning to help with processes like DNA sequences, drug discovery, and tumor detection.

4. Energy production. This is when we use machine learning to help with price and load forecasting.

5. Manufacturing, aerospace, and automotive. This is when we are going to use machine learning to help out with processes that include predictive maintenance.

6. Natural language processing. This is when we will use the idea of machine learning to help with applications of voice recognition, like what we see on many smartphones.

Machine learning algorithms are helpful because they are going to find some of the natural patterns that are already in the large amount of data a company holds onto, and then it can generate the right insights while helping you to make good predictions and decisions in the process. These algorithms are going to be used each day in order to make critical decisions in things like energy load forecasting, stock trading, and medical diagnosis, to name a few.

A good example of this is with the media. Many media sites are already relying on the algorithms that come with machine learning in order to sift through the millions of options to provide the movie or song recommendations for you. Retailers have been using these algorithms in order to gain some good insights on their customers and the behavior for purchasing that they see there, and then they can provide good recommendations and make changes that improve their bottom line.

We also need to consider some of the times when machine learning can be helpful. You will need to bring out machine learning, and some of the algorithms that come with it, any time that you would like to work with a task that is more complex, or you would like to solve a problem that needs a large amount of data, and there are quite a few variables that go with it, but there isn't an equation or a formula that exists to handle this.

For example, some of the times when you will want to work with machine learning to help your business to grow will include some of the following:

1. Looking at handwritten rules and equations that are going to be too hard to do manually. This could include some of the processes, like speech recognition or facial recognition.

2. When the rules of the task you want to complete are going to change on you all the time; this might include something like transaction records or fraud detection.

3. When the nature of the data that you would like to use keeps changing, and you want to make sure that the program you are using will be able to adapt. This is going to include some processes like predicting the trends in shopping, forecasting energy demand, and automated trading.

Machine learning is going to work with three types of techniques or methods that you want to work with based on the kind of data you want to work with. The types of machine learning that you are able to work with will include supervised machine learning and unsupervised machine learning. Let's dive into both of these and see how they can work to our benefit.

The first type of machine learning that we are able to take a look at is known as supervised learning. This type of learning is going to be able to build up a model we can use that can make good predictions based on evidence that we have, in the presence of uncertainty. The algorithm that fits this mold is going to be able to take a known set of input data, along with the responses that we already know about the data or the output. It can then train the model that you have to generate some reasonable predictions when it receives new data along the way.

You are going to work with supervised machine learning if you have the known data for the kind of output that you would like to predict. This process involves you providing the right examples to the model so that it can learn. You provide the input, and the output learns from this, and then it can make good predictions based on what it has learned as time goes on, and it receives some new information or input.

There are two types of techniques that are going to work when you want to use supervised machine learning in order to develop your own predictive models. The first one is going to be a classification technique. This kind is going to help us to predict a discrete response. Some examples of this are when you want the model to estimate whether the email is spam or a genuine email. Classification models are going to be able to classify the data that is used as inputs into different categories. Typical applications are going to include things like credit scoring, speech recognition, and medical imaging.

You can work with classification any time that you can take the data and separate it, categorize it, and tag it into specific classes or groups. For example, applications that are going to use handwriting recognition is going to use classification in order to help the program recognize different numbers and letters. When we work with things like image segmentation or object detection, you are going to be working more with the unsupervised machine learning that we will look at in a bit.

There are a variety of different types of algorithms that a data scientist is able to work with when it comes to doing supervised learning on classification problems. Some of the types of algorithms that fit into this will include neural networks, logistic regression, Naïve Bayes, K-nearest neighbors, decision trees, and support vector machines.

Likewise, we can work with the regression techniques. These can predict responses that are continuous, like a change in the temperature of a certain area, or the fluctuations that show up in the demand for power. Some of the typical applications of the regression techniques are going to include algorithmic trading and electricity load forecasting, to name a few.

You will want to work with some of these regression techniques if you are working with a data range or if the nature of the response that you would like to get out of that data is going to be a real number, such as a time unit failure on your equipment, or the temperature. Some of the regression algorithms that you are likely to work with could be stepwise regression, nonlinear and linear model, and adaptive neur0-fuzzy learning.

The next type of machine learning that we need to focus on for a few minutes is the idea of unsupervised machine learning. This one is not going to need the examples in order to make things work. Instead, it is going to work on its own in order to find the hidden structures that are found in the data. You can use this kind of learning to figure out what inferences are in the set of data consisting of input data that doesn't come with labeled responses.

The most common technique that you can use with unsupervised machine learning is clustering. This clustering is going to be used to help with data analysis that is more exploratory in nature. This means that the clustering is going to help us to find groupings or hidden patterns that are in the data some of the applications that we can see with a cluster analysis will include object recognition, market research, and gene sequence analysis.

A good example of this can be seen with some of the work that a cell phone company partakes in. Let's say that this company would like to optimize the areas where they build up new phone towers. To do this, they can work with unsupervised machine learning in order to estimate the number of clusters of people who rely on these towers, and where these individuals are residing. They can't put up a tower were one or two customers are located, but if they see that there is a significant number of people in an area, it may be a good idea to place a tower there.

A phone can only talk to one of the towers at a time, so the team is going to use the algorithms of clustering to design the best placement of the cell towers, optimizing the reception of the signal for the groups, or in this case the clusters of their customers.

Just like with supervised machine learning, there are also a few different types of clustering that you are able to work with to complete your work with unsupervised machine learning. Some of the options that we can work with include self-organizing maps, the hidden Markov models, Gaussian mixture models, and hierarchical clustering.

The third type of machine learning that you can work with is known as *reinforcement machine learning*. This one is often one that is forgotten or combined with unsupervised machine learning because the two are so similar. Rather than relying on unlabeled data on its own, reinforcement learning focuses on the idea of trial and error. As it makes errors, it will learn what not to do and will make some changes. If it makes the right decisions, it is going to form some strong connections that will help it to do better the next time it encounters the same example.

How can I Decide Which is the Correct Algorithm to Use?

The next thing to focus on is how you can choose the right algorithm that you can work with. This can be an overwhelming thing to work with. There are going to be a lot of different algorithms that you can work with here to make predictions, both with supervised and unsupervised machine learning, and each of them will take on a different approach when it comes to learning.

There is no best method to work with, and no one size fits all. Finding the right algorithm in some cases is going to be all about trial and error. And even those who have been doing this kind of work for a longer period of time can't always tell whether or not one algorithm is the best one, at least until they try it out.

Often the selection that you make with picking out the right algorithm is going to depend on the type and the size of the data that you are working with, the insights that you are trying to get out of that data, and how you would like to use the insights that you receive. Some of the basic things that you can remember and consider when you are working with these algorithms, and when you are stuck trying to decide between supervised and unsupervised machine learning will include:

> 1. You want to go with supervised learning at any time that it is best to train your model to make a prediction. You could use it to help you work with a future value that is a continuous variable such as the stock price or a temperature. It can also work with classification, such as identifying the make of the car from footage found in a webcam.

> 2. You want to go with unsupervised machine learning if you would like to explore your data, and you are looking to train the model in order to find a good representation that is internal, such as taking all of the data that you brought in and then splitting that data into some clusters.

> 3.

How Machine Learning Can Assist in Making Predictions

Many of the different types of algorithms that come with machine learning can come into play and will help you to make some smart decisions in the process. These algorithms are set up to handle a lot of the information and the data that you are collecting and can make predictions for you. In fact, this is one of the main things that machine learning is able to do!

With machine learning, we already recognize that it is really hard for us to go through and sort through all of the data that we collect for the business. When millions of data points come at us all of the time, from social media, a website, survey results, or something else, and this is just too much for a single person to go through, or even a team to go through. It would take too long, and since there is a constant stream of this data, it is impossible for them to come up with relevant information and decisions in a timely manner.

You can certainly try it, but by the time the person actually went through all of that information and saw the trends or the patterns, the information would be old, and they would be way behind the competition. It is much better to make your decisions based on intuition and business sense and see what results you get, rather than spending time manually going through all the data that is available.

Rather than doing this, you can work with some of the algorithms that come with machine learning to look through the information. These algorithms are able to take that information and go through it quickly, providing you with a good prediction and all the possible outcomes that can happen as well based on the data that you feed in. While it could take years for an individual to attempt to keep up with this information and see the trends, the algorithm can get this done really quickly, and could keep up with the constant stream that the company gets with the data.

There are many different types of machine learning that you can work with and a bunch of algorithms that fit into the three types that we talked about earlier including supervised, unsupervised, and reinforcement learning. The type of algorithm that you decide to use when it comes to machine learning will make a big difference in the results that you see, and often it depends on the kind of data that you are using, and the end results that you are hoping to get out of it in the process.

If you work with machine learning in the proper manner, you will be able to set up a model with the chosen algorithm that will then be able to handle all of the data as it comes in. Some algorithms can take in a steady stream of data as it comes in, and others need you to manually go in and provide the data at the times when you want the new predictions. You can then set up the model so that it handles all your data in a consistent manner while dealing with some of the other types of analysis that we have talked about in this guidebook already.

Most of the industries that are out there that are already working with large amounts of data are going to be able to recognize the kind of value that they would get with using the technology that comes with machine learning. By being able to actually get through this data and glean some good insights from it, and being able to do this close to real-time, the company is then able to work in a more efficient manner in order to gain a big advantage of others in their same industry.

And this is the beauty of working with machine learning. We are able to do things that may have seemed impossible in the pat are possible now with the help of machine learning. Businesses that are handling more data than ever before are finding the value of working with machine learning to help them get their work done. They can get through this information faster than would be possible with a person looking through it on their own, and can give them that competitive edge over others.

There are a lot of different companies that will be able to benefit from a program that can run on machine learning. Some of the different industries that are already using this kind of technology will include financial services, government, health care, retail, oil and gas, transportation, and more.

The Prediction Explanation

Traditionally, when we look at some of the models found in machine learning, they are not going to provide us insights into why or how the model arrived at the outcome that it did. This is going to make it a bit harder to explain in an objective manner the decisions that are made, and the actions that it took based on these models. Prediction explanations are going to avoid the black box syndrome by describing which characteristics or feature variables, are going to have the biggest impact on the outcome that you will see with the outcomes of the models.

When we need to know the reasons that are behind the outcome we see with a model, and this background is as important as the outcomes themselves, the prediction explanations are going to come in and uncover some of the factors that can come and contribute to the outcomes. We may not get the algorithm to come in and tell us exactly what it is doing all of the time, but we can get it to help us see some of the most probable steps that were taken in the process.

It can be frustrating not to know the real reasons why an algorithm is going to do one task over another, or how it came up with the prediction or the outcome that it presents to us. This is not good for business either. How are we supposed to know if the result that we got is the real one that we need, or if it is one that we need to be worried about because some outliers got in the way? Working with the prediction explanation, along with the algorithm that we have, can make a world of difference.

For example, banks are already using models to help them determine whether it is a good idea to approve a loan for a particular customer or not. These financial institutions are able to use what is known as prediction explanations in order to gain some insight into why an application was rejected or accepted. Then the loan officer would be able to see whether the reasons make sense or if something is going wrong with the information.

With the insight that the prediction explanation provides, it is easier for the bank to develop some models that will help them comply with any of the regulations they have. They can also come up with a model that can explain the outcomes of the model to their stakeholders, and a model that will identify some of the high impact factors to help the bank stay on track with some of their business strategies.

Machine learning can be one of the best topics that you are able to use in order to get the algorithms that come with it to work well and to ensure that you are going to get a good idea of how the prediction happened in the first place. This may seem like something that isn't as big of a deal, but before we base a decision on what the algorithm shows to us, we need to see how it is showing us the predictions and how it comes up with the conclusion that it presented to you as well. The prediction explanation is going to help you to make this all work and will ensure that you are actually making smart and accurate decisions based on your data.

Chapter 8: How to Avoid Prediction Traps, Avoid Bias, and Make the Best Predictions

As we have explored in this guidebook, there are a lot of things that you are able to do with predictive analysis, and you may be surprised at all of the different methods that you can bring on board in order to see some amazing results. While it is important to learn as much about the benefits of this predictive analysis as possible, and we do go in-depth about this more in the next chapter, there are a few things that we need to be wary of, and learn how to watch out for, if we truly want to make predictive models that are able to help us out.

While many companies are ready to jump on board with the ideas of the predictive analysis because they like all of the opportunities that are presented with it, and all that this is going to be able to help them out with, we do need to focus a bit on being careful about some of the traps and the biases that can sneak into our models. Sometimes we know those biases and traps are there because we set them to get the answers that we want. If this is something that you plan to do from the start, then just stop now and don't do any more work. That will just be a waste of your time, energy, and resources because you already know the answer you would like to get.

Often though, the traps and biases are going to sneak their way into the model, and we didn't even realize what was going on in the first place. This can be just as dangerous, even though we don't realize what is going on, because we are allowing our data to be tainted with, and this can harm the end result that we end up getting.

Our goal here is actually to learn what is inside of all that data. Approaching it with a clear and open mind, rather than focusing on what we think should be there, is the key to helping us actually learn something new. And you may find that during this practice, you are going to find a lot of useful information and insights that you were not expecting to find in the first place. That is part of the fun and the excitement of the predictive analysis. It allows you to learn something new, which can go a long way in ensuring that you see some good results for your business.

With this said, we now need to take some time to use our predictive analytics, but first, we have to focus on some of the ways that we can avoid prediction traps and any of the biases that we may try to get into the models so that we can look at the information with new eyes, and glean some useful information out of it in no time at all.

How to Avoid some of the Traps and Biases

You will find that predictive analytics can yield amazing results. The lift that you can see in your business is going to be achieved when you base some of your future decisions on the observed patterns that are found in historical data, and we find that this can far outweigh anything that can be achieved when we rely on anecdotal events or our gut feelings. These decisions are going to be made using evidence and facts to back them up, which can ensure that you will see the best results.

There are a lot of examples that will show us the possible lift that we are able to see through all of the different industries, but one test that was done recently that is done in the retail sector will show that applying stable predictive models was able to give a huge increase, up to fivefold, in the take up of a product when we were comparing it to a random sample. And if this weren't enough to convince us that this was a good thing to spend our time on, we have to admit that there wouldn't be as much focus on predictive analysis, and some of the cool things that we can do with it and machine learning, if it wasn't helping businesses in many different manners, and if it was not providing these businesses with some good results.

Of course, we can't assume that these predictive models are going to be accurate all of the time, and we have to take the necessary precautions to make sure that we are using them in the proper manner. They can be sensitive to change sometimes, and they have a propensity to make sudden shifts up and down based on the results that we put in and the kind of data that we are going to use for the model. Having someone who is able to handle the information and the model, and who will use it in the proper manner is going to be imperative to make this process work.

The commoditizing of machine learning is going to be useful because it helps data science become more accessible to the non-data scientists of the world than we have seen in the past. But with this in mind, we have to make sure to avoid some of the common pitfalls that come with predictive analytics, in order to keep the models performing as expected.

We like to think in many cases that the predictive model is going to be able to solve all of our problems. And sometimes, we use it to prove the hypothesis that we already have in our minds. These are just two of the pitfalls that come with this kind of analysis, and it can really cause some issues with the model you are using. Learning what these pitfalls are all about, and how to avoid them can make a big difference in the accuracy and efficiency that you will see from these models. Some of the most common pitfalls that we may see with our predictive models, and that we need to watch out for includes:

The first bias and trap that we need to watch out for are making some assumptions that are incorrect about the underlying data we use for training. Rushing into this process and making assumptions on the training data may seem to save us sense time, but it is going to lead to some troubles. As a data analyst and someone who really wants to get at the root of the information found in your data, it is much better to take some time to understand the data and then find the trends I the distributions, the outliers, and the missing values.

It is also possible that the data analyst is going to try and work with low volumes. This may seem like the best option to work with a new model, but it is going to harm your model and will not make it as strong as you want. Low volumes are actually meant to be your unhappy place in this process. These low volumes are going to lead to models that are unreliable, unstable, and statistically weak.

This means that you need to take some time to gather and clean off more data before you work on your models. This ensures that you get some strong models out of the process because the training data that you are working with will make it easier to get a strong and reliable model that you are able to use to make predictions.

Next on the list is going to be the trap of overfitting things. What this means is that you are creating a new model that has a lot of branches. This may seem like a good idea to have more options and more branches because it seems to provide us with a lot of better discrimination when it comes to the target variable. But when we bring this over to the real world, we will find that all that it does is introduce too much noise into our model, and makes the model less reliable and accurate in the process.

The training data is something that we need to spend time on, and we have to make sure that we are eliminating this training bias as much as possible. For example, you only took the time to offer a certain product to the millennials in your target audience. With this, you will find that the millennials are going to come in really strongly on this model. Since they did not get a choice to work with, it was hard to figure out what they would actually behave like if they had some choices.

We also need to look at the test data and the training data. One of the biggest mistakes that can happen when you work with both is that you add in the test data with your *training data*. This has led to a few fails because it gives the impression that your model is the best one out there, and it is going to perform fantastically. But in reality, when you do this, you will find that the model you want to work with does not work all that well, and it is actually a broken model.

In the world of predictive analytics, if the results you receive seem to be too good to be true, then it is often a good idea to go back through and see what this is all about. Spending some more time and money to validate the results you get when they seem too good to be true and even getting another opinion to look over your work to see what mistakes may have been made will ensure that you get a model that is going actually to work for you.

Companies who want to work with predictive analysis also need to learn how to be creative with the data that they are provided. If the creativity is kept out of the mix, then this is going to be another trap that we fall into that is going to harm the model we want to focus on. You may find that the predictive model that you are working with is going to be improved quite a bit when you can add in a few clever features or characteristics that are going to explain, in a much better and clearer method, some of the trends that show up in the data.

There are too many times that a data scientist will play by the book, and won't work with any sort of creativity in the process. They will just take the data that they are provided, not spending enough time considering some of the features they could add which are more creative. This creativity is going to help add some more strength to the models you are creating, adding in the strength in ways that even improving the algorithm will not be able to achieve all on its own either.

We also have to remember that we can't expect our machines to understand business. There are a lot of cool things that we are able to do with our machines, and when we add in artificial intelligence and machine learning to the mix, we can teach our computers to handle a lot of the same things that humans can. But we have to understand that right now at least; our machines are not able to understand business or how to handle it.

Machines - as of right now - are not able to figure out what the business problem is and how it can best tackle the problem for you. This is not always something that is easy to understand, and we often need to give it some careful thought. Businesses spend a lot of time talking out decisions and researching it before making any decisions, and this is not something that we can teach a computer how to do right now. Expecting that the machine is going to come in and handle all the problems that we have, without any interactions from us at all, is going to set us up for failure.

Another thing that we need to consider here is that we don't want to use the wrong metric to measure out the performance of the model. Let's say as an example that out of 10,000 cases, you only have two fraudulent cases, and the rest are just fine. If the performance metric that was used in the training of the model was completely straightforward accuracy, the model is going to attempt to maximize the accuracy that it sees.

Thus, if the model is going to predict that all the 10,000 cases are not fraud, then the model would come in with a 99.8 percent accuracy. This may seem really great, but it is not going to serve us much purpose when it comes to seeing whether or not some of the cases had fraud or not. It simply means that it identified 99.98 percent of the non-fraud instances in the correct manner for the company.

When you are working with rare event modeling, of which the fraud example above is going to help us out, it is best if you can skip the accuracy metric that we used, and instead go with an alternative approach to help us figure out what is going on here.

Using plain linear models when the interaction needs to be non-linear.

This is most likely to happen when you would like to build up a binary classifier, and you choose the logistic regression for this method - when, the relationship that shows up between the features is not going to be linear. In the case above, working with a model that is tree-based or the support vector machines will work better.

This is where it is helpful to know more about the algorithms that you want to use, so you can make sure you are not using the wrong ones on your data. Not knowing which methods can be applicable to the problem you are trying to handle can result in models that are not very good, and the predictions that you get out of them will not be accurate either.

Next on the list is going to be the outliers. These outliers are usually going to deserve at least a little bit of your attention, or they should be ignored. There are going to be a few of these models that are going to be really sensitive to the outliers, and if you use these algorithms, and you forget to take them out, or at least cater to them, then this leads to some bad performance in the model that you want to work with.

You also need to be careful about regularizations without any standardizations. Many of the companies who choose to work with this predictive analysis are not going to be aware of some of the redundancy of applying regularization to the features of the model, without first going through and standardizing the data to ensure that the data is on the same scale.

If you choose to do this, then the regularization would end up as biased because it is going to penalize the features that are on a smaller scale that you want to use here. This could be a bad thing because it kicks out some of the information that you need, and can make it hard to really see the information and the predictions that you need in the process.

As a company, you need to make sure that you take into account the real-time scoring environment that is present. Sometimes a company using the predictive model is going to get distracted by building the model that is the most perfect. They want everything to be in place and ready to go at the right times (and the right places) all the time.

This is a great goal to have, but it is not realistic. When it comes to deployment, when we work on a model that we want to make perfect, this often becomes so complex that the model can't be integrated into a system that is operational. You do not want to spend so much time on a model, working to make sure that everything is perfect, just to find out that it won't work, and you need to make changes again.

We also need to not fall into the trap of using some characteristics that will not be there in the future, usually because of some operational reasons. One thing that the company may identify is some predictive characteristics, like gender, but because of regulations, you can't use this kind of field to help out with modeling. You also will find that it can't be used in capturing the field that has been suspended and will be available in the future for use in the model.

The final trap that we are going to take a look at is not considering some of the implications of the real world with the model, and some of the possible fallout that could happen when we do one of these analytics. One example of this is the retailer Target. They made headlines a few years ago when a reporter from the New York Times brought it to the attention of the public that the analytics models that Target used were able to predict the pregnancy of a teenager based on how they were shopping on the store.

What this can tell us is just because we can find out some information, doesn't necessarily mean that we should. Yes, there was probably enough data information that was going through their system that they could find out this information based on the age of the customer and what they were shopping for, such as a pregnancy test, but did they really need to know this? Most likely not. It is important that you spend some time looking at the right information, the information that you need to know to grow your business, rather than just collecting information because you can.

There is a lot of useful information that someone can glean when they decide to use predictive analysis in their business. These companies are already gathering a large amount of information on a regular basis already, so why not use it to provide better customer service, and to beat out the competition. But we do need to remember that taking care of the information that we use, and not falling into the traps and biases that come with that information can be important as well.

Chapter 9: Top Reasons to Implement predictive analysis

We have spent some time talking about the various benefits that come with using one of these predictive analytics in your business, but we need to take this a bit further to see how things will go when you actually implement it into your business model. There are a lot of different options when it comes to the way that you will use the predictive analysis, and we have spent some time discussing many of them as we worked through this guidebook. With this in mind, it is time for us to look more in-depth at why you and your business should be using these predictive analytics in the first place.

First, let's take a look at the world of marketing. Marketers are always thinking about new and more efficient ways that they can engage with their customers. According to an insights case study from Forbes called "How Predictive Analytics Helps Cox Communication Tune into Customers," employing the predictive analytics to gain a deeper insight into some of the trends with the consumer has proven to be more successful for many companies, not only for Cox Communication, but for other options as well.

The telecommunications industry is going to be prone to a higher amount of turnover from their customers, mainly because the costs for switching are slim to none, and often it ends up saving them a lot of money. Companies that are in this industry are going to look for new ways to differentiate themselves from their competitors in the hopes of retaining some new customers. It is possible that if predictive analytics is used properly, it is going to help these companies to find the right solutions that will allow them to understand better, and then retain their customers. It can even help them to bring in a new customer in a more effective manner.

It is believed that there are five top reasons why a company would want to use these predictive analytics to help them out in different areas. The top reasons that come with predictive analysis will be predicting trends, understanding the customer, drive decision making that is more strategic, to improve the performance of the business, and to predict behavior. Let's take a closer look at how these can all be done and why a business would want to spend their time on each of these.

Predicting Trends that are Coming Soon

One of the first things that businesses are going to do when they work on predictive analysis is figuring out some of the upcoming trends that are in the market. The companies that are able to learn about the trends first, and stick with these trends, are the ones that will be able to beat out the competition and actually gain a new corner of the market.

Wouldn't you rather be the company that comes out in a brand new market, or comes up with the newest product that everyone wants, first? Or do you want to watch other companies do these things, and then try to follow after them, hoping to get some form of the market in the process? Using the predictive analysis is one of the ways that you can ensure that you will be ahead of the competition, rather than trying to play catchup and trying to get some of the markets that is leftover.

Let's look at an example. Amazon came out several years ago with Kindle, a device that would allow you to read any book from their library - anywhere you wanted to go. This made it easier for customers to have an easy way to take books around with them, and they could easily sit and enjoy the books without having to carry a whole pile along with them. This was a revolutionary idea, one of a kind, and it is likely that Amazon used something like predictive analysis to help come up with this idea, and found that their customers would really enjoy a product like this.

Amazon got to reap the rewards of this and was one of the first to release this to the market. Everyone else had to try and catch up in order to get obtain some market share. While it is true that there are other readers out there, Amazon is still considered number one with this, and the other options had to really struggle to make theirs unique and different in order to stand out and get some of the customers.

Your business can benefit from doing this kind of thing as well; you just need to learn how to collect the right data, and then perform the right kind of analysis on it to see what your customers want, and what some of the new trends will be. If you can spot these trends and understand what the customer wants before anyone else in the industry does, you can easily step in and really make a product that is first of its kind.

Sometimes, the product is not going to be as big as the Kindle Reader, and maybe it won't change up the whole industry, but it could help you to get a new market for your company, or reach a new demographics before others do. Any kind of good trend that you can jump on first that gets you ahead of the competition is going to do wonders for helping your company to grow and to thrive in the long run.

Add some Artificial Intelligence to the Mix

Artificial intelligence, often referred to as "AI," is an area of computer science. Which can emphasize the creation of systems and intelligent machines and can work - and often react - like what we see with humans. A lot of different computer activities use AI, and are designed to help with planning, learning, problem-solving, and speech recognition.

Basically, when we are working with artificial intelligence, we ~~are going to~~ work with a branch of the larger field of computer science. In this particular part, we are looking at a process that can create intelligent machines, ones that are able to think and act on their own. And because of the power that comes with these systems, it has easily become an essential part of the technology industry as more and more businesses and companies work to use this along the way.

Research that has been done on AI is specialized and highly technical. This could be due to the nature of how artificial intelligence works and all of the different parts that come with it. Some of the core problems that come with the AI include programming the computer for a certain trait. Including the ability to move and manipulate a variety of objects, learning, perception, planning, knowledge, problem-solving, and reasoning.

Knowledge will be power when it comes to working with artificial intelligence, and this knowledge engineering is going to be part of the core of research in this field. Machines are often able to learn how to act and react as a human does, but only if they have been given enough information about how the world works and how they should behave.

The next thing that we need to explore here is why artificial intelligence is so important. Why do we need to spend so much time going through some of the basics that come with artificial intelligence, and why is this a topic that matters at all? Artificial intelligence is starting to take over the world, and learning how to use it for needs can make a big difference in how well companies perform for the customers, and so much more. There are a number of reasons why artificial intelligence would be an important thing to learn how to do. These reasons are going to include:

AI is able to automate some of the repetitive learning that goes on and can help lead to more discoveries through data. AI is going to be different than what we see with hardware-driven robotic automation. Instead of having to go through and automating some of the manual tasks, AI is going to work on frequent, computerized, and high volume tasks in a reliable manner and without getting tired. To get this particular type of automation going, human inquiry is still going to be essential when it comes to getting that system set up in the proper manner and asking the questions that are needed.

In addition, AI is going to make sure that a product you already have is going to have more intelligence added to it. In most cases, AI is not going to be sold with the help of an individual application. Instead, the products that you are already using will be improved with the help of AI. Many different smart machines can be combined together with all of the data the company holds onto to make sure that the technology is improved, no matter which field it is in.

AI is going to be able to adapt through the progressive learning algorithms so that the data gets to do the programming. AI is able to find any of the regularities or the structure in data so that the algorithm is able to gain a new skill. This algorithm is going to turn into either a predictor or a classifier. So, just like we see the algorithm being able to teach itself the right steps to playing chess, it is also able to use this kind of idea in order to recommend which product the customer should purchase next.

Visualizations Can Make It Easier to Show Results to Others

While a data scientist is going to spend their time going through all of that data, and trying to come up with some of the patterns and trends that are found inside, it is going to be the business owners and the shareholders who really need to know more about the information and can use that data to make predictions. The data scientist can make all of the algorithms and models that they want, but if no one outside of that field is able to understand the information, then it pretty much becomes useless.

Many data scientists need to not only gather the data and then find the trends, but they must make sure that they can take that information and put it into some kind of graphic form to see results. There are a few different methods and models that you are able to use to make sure that this visualization works, such as a chart, a pie chart, a histogram, or a line chart, but you need to make sure that it matches up with the information that you would like to show off.

Sure, you could just present the findings and all of the numbers to others, but this is not the most effective way for them to understand what is inside. These visualizations will allow anyone who wants to, to just look at the information and the findings in a glance, rather than having to read through it all and try to figure out what is there.

Picking the right visualization to go with the work that you are trying to do can be imperative. It will ensure that you are actually representing the data in the right manner, rather than making things worse. You can experiment with a few different options that fit here in order to see which one seems to represent the data that you have the best.

Of course, it is fine to add in the actual information and the predictions that were made to create those visuals. This allows anyone who would like to check your information and data to go back through it and give you some results. But the visual is going to be helpful because it gives us all the information at a glance, and the predictive analysis - if it is done in the proper manner - can do this for us as well.

Drive Decisions that are Better for the Company

Some of the best decisions that you can make for your company are going to come after performing predictive analysis. These decisions are going to be based on facts rather than just a guess, even if it is an educated guess. Sometimes, the lack of knowledge that we have is surprising, and this is going to harm us if we are not careful about what we are doing.

In the past, there wasn't such a thing as big data or any of the analysis that we have talked about so far in this guidebook. We were not able to pull up data from pretty much any source and then use that information to guide the decisions that we made. Instead, people would have to ask for opinions from others and use some of their own knowledge of the business to determine the right course of action to take.

Sometimes, the business owner would be good at what they were doing, and they would make predictions that we're able to move their business forward. And the longer the individual was in business, the better chance they had of making good predictions as well. But even those who have been in the business for a long time may find that they can fail and run into trouble if they are not careful, and without the proper data behind them to help guide those decisions, it is possible for anyone to fail.

With this in mind, using predictive analysis is going to help with these decisions. Whether you have been in the business for a long period of time, or you are brand new to the industry, these analysis give you the hard facts and data that you need to really see what is going on with your customers, with your business, and even with the industry, so you can make the decisions that are right for your needs.

With this analysis, you have the facts behind you. And often, there are a lot of facts that show up thanks to all the collection methods and the storage solutions for gaining and holding onto this information. You can then go through some of the steps that we talk about in this guidebook and learn what information is hidden in that data, and make the decisions that your business needs based on this data.

While using your intuition in some cases can still be a good idea, this is not something that we need to rely on as much any longer. Working with big data and a good analysis that can keep up in real-time to this big data, will ensure that you can really take care of the things you need to in business, and can lead you to see some amazing results in the process.

Understand Customers

One way that a lot of companies are going to choose to work with the predictive analysis is in order to understand their customers better. The more that you know about your customers, the easier it is to make the right products for them, enhance some of your current products for them, answer their questions, market to them, and so much more. A company that knows nothing about their customers, or who acts like they barely care about their customer is the company that is going to fail.

This predictive analysis is going to ensure that the company is going to make their customers happy, as long as they really pay attention to what the information is saying, and they are willing to take the right steps to make it happen. Maybe they gather some information from social media that their customers would like more options to choose from, or they wish it were easier to get ahold of the company. The customers may make complaints about the time it takes to ship the items, or that they feel that the item is not really much different than what the competitor has.

While every company would like to think they offer the best product, and it is hard to hear negatives about your product and the hard work that you are putting in, this is a part of life. Being able to improve your business means that you need to listen to the complaints that they are presenting to you, and then try to fix them as well as possible. This doesn't mean that every complaint is reasonable, or that you have to try and make everyone happy. But often, when you bring in some of the analysis and look through the data, you will start to notice that there are some common trends that show up, and you may realize that maybe it is time to make some changes.

You can also use this data to learn more about some of the demographics that come with your customer base and create better marketing campaigns for them as well. The more that you can learn about the demographics of your customers, the easier it is to reach them. Knowing their age, their interests, their jobs, their hobbies where they live, what kind of family situation they have, their gender, etc., makes it easier to send out personalized messages to everyone and can increase your sales.

Doing predictive analysis over your target audience is going to ensure you gather the right kind of data that serves to inform you about your customers. Shooting in the dark, or assuming that you know your customer without any research, is basically throwing money down the drain. You may be surprised after doing your research that your target demographics are not what you think, or that there may be another kind of group you can reach in addition to your current audience, to increase your profits overall.

One thing you should note is some of the outliers in your data. Sometimes, the outliers are not going to be that important. They will include a few people who want some suggestions that just aren't possible for your business and how it is set up, or they may include those few customers who had a bad experience with your product. If you look at the outliers and see that it is just a few people, and it seems that by making those people happy, it is going to cost too much or alienate the other customers the majority, then it is fine to ignore them.

But it is still important to look at these outliers. Sometimes, they can show us something new, and alert us to a new trend or a new idea that could help put us above the competition. Perhaps you see that most of your demographics fit in the 25-30-year-old range, but then you look at the outliers and find that there is a significant, albeit smaller group, that fits into another range. If these outliers are all in the same age group, then this could be a potential sign of a new demographic group for you, and it may be worth your time to start marketing to them.

This could be the sign idea with a new product idea that you have. Maybe once you see that you have a different demographic, you decide to do some more research and find out which product, in particular, is going to really help them, and may draw in more people from that demographic. Maybe you will start to change up some of your marketing to include ads for this different demographic as well.

Often, this new area is going to be hidden if you just ignore your information and all of that data you are taking in. It is not going to be near large enough to push out your main demographics or what you are currently doing right now, but it is still large enough to show you some potential if you see it. And because you did the predictive analysis, you may be able to reach this demographic before some of the other people in your industry do, allowing you to make the most money here and see the best results.

Improve the performance of the business

Many times businesses will try to use the predictive analysis in order to improve their overall performance. They want to not only provide some better customer service, but they want to avoid times when their machines are down and not working, cut out costs of production, and not overwork the employees they have. If you gather up the right kind of data and learn how to use predictive analysis on it, it becomes infinitely easier to figure out how to improve all of these areas, making your business save money, reduce waste, and more efficient in the long term.

The first benefit here is that predictive analysis is going to help the business to save money. When they are able to use the analysis to figure out where things are too expensive, or how to become more efficient, that will automatically cut down on a lot of the costs that they are dealing with. When they can prevent things from going to waste as often when they can prevent machines going down all of the time, and when they get a chance to see what parts of the process are necessary and what parts are not, it is much easier to cut down on costs, and improve the bottom line.

Another benefit is that the business can use predictive analysis to provide better customer service. They will learn what their customers really want, be able to find new and innovative ways to deal with their customers, and can ensure that everything is taken care of in an orderly and timely fashion, something that may have been difficult to do in the past.

We can also look at this in terms of warranties and the amount that is being spent on products that are returned. When a customer gets a defective product, they are going to return it. This costs the business, either in refunding the money or in replacing it, plus all that goes into handling these claims. When predictive analysis is brought on board, looking at ways to reduce the defective products so that they save money from here as well. (This is something that also goes into Six Sigma a bit, so if this is your problem, it is another good topic to explore.)

Predictive analysis can also come into play in terms of monitoring the machines that help make your product and learning when it is likely that a part on the machine is going to wear out or break. When we are able to figure this out ahead of time, it is much easier to schedule the repair or the replacement ahead of time and get that fixed during the night or another downtime for the company. This keeps the production line moving, rather than losing a lot of time and money trying to get things fixed after the part breaks.

Predict Behavior

The fifth benefit that comes with performing predictive analysis is that the business can use this in order to predict the behavior of their customers, and their competitors. This is going to make it easier for them to create marketing for your customers, find the best products to send out to the market, and make sure that you are going to be able to be ahead of the competition all of the time.

First, you can use this kind of analysis in order to predict the kind of behavior that your customers are going to showcase when it comes to your business. This can help you to see what products to release, hopefully, before the rest of the competition steps in and does the same thing. You want to know how they view your product, how they will use your product, and any other behavior that is going to be important when it comes to your business in particular.

Predicting behavior is not always an easy process to work with for many people. It is going to be hard for a business just to figure out what behaviors they are likely to show. And we are not asking you just to make random predictions without help. Instead, we are looking at you to take all of the data that you have been able to collect over some period of time, and then perform a good predictive analysis on this data, opening up a lot of information and insights that can make this possible.

Your predictions may not be accurate all of the time. There are some people who will stray off the path and not behave in the way that you are predicting all of the time. These will be known as the outliers, and it is something that you will see on a regular basis. The point here is to figure out what the general behavior of your customers is like and then work from there to see how you can best serve them to grow your business.

There are a lot of benefits of using predictive analysis for every business, no matter what kind of industry you are in. This can help you to learn so much about the customers you are working with and the competition you have to go against. With all of that data you are bringing in, it makes sense that you would want to do an analysis of it and figure out what trends and insights are inside for your benefit. Make sure to check out these great benefits that go along with predictive analysis to see why your business would see some improvements in the way your business performs.

Chapter 10: The Top Steps to Help You Create Your Own Predictive Analysis Model

Now that we have spent a good deal of time talking about what predictive analysis is all about and some of the benefits that come from using this kind of analysis in your own business, it is time for us to take this a bit further and look at creating your own predictive analysis model to use any way that you would like. It is fine to have some of the theories behind this analysis to help you get started, but now it is time for us to actually put it to good use and see what steps we have to take to create and implement this kind of model into our own business.

A successful predictive analytics project is one that we are able to execute step by step. As you start to become more immersed in the details of the project, there are a few milestones and a few steps that you will need to follow along the way. Some of these are going to include:

1. Define your business objectives

How are you supposed to create a model that works, if you don't know what you want it to accomplish or how it is supposed to match up with the business you are running? You need to have some clear goals, and some clear objectives, to help you see the best results in this process.

The project here is going to start out with a business objective that is well-defined. The model needs to be able to address the question that your business has. Clearly stating out the objective that you want to follow at the start of the project, and then keep this in mind the whole time you do the work, can make it easier for you to define what the scope of your project will be. It is also one of the best ways for you to test to see how successful the project is from the beginning, and can help you see if another method is needed, long before you get to the end of the project and waste a lot of time.

2. Preparing the Data

From here, we are going to use some historical data in order to train the model that we want to use. The data here is usually going to be scattered across a variety of sources. You can gather the data anywhere you would like, and often the thing that you want to measure will determine where the data will come from. Some companies rely on the information they get from social media. Some will send our surveys, will collect data from how their customer's shop, or will look to research that has been done on their industry to provide them with some insights.

Since you are getting the data from so many different sources, it is likely that you will need to take some time to cleanse and prepare the data. Data can come in with duplicate records, which can skew the results that you get and some outliers. And depending on the kind of analysis that you want to do, and the objectives for your business, you need to decide whether it is a good idea to remove or keep these things.

Along the way, you may find that your data has some values missing, it may need some kind of transformation to help it to work, and it could be used to generate some derived attributes that will have more predictive power for your objective. Keep in mind that many times, the quality that you have in your data will determine the quality of the model that you produce, so spend some time preparing the data to get the best results.

3. Sampling the Data

At this point, we need to be able to split up our data so that it is found in two different sets. For this, we need to have a set for training, and then a set for testing out the model. Both of these are important because they allow the model to learn what you want, and then you can test it out to make sure that the model learned the way that it was supposed to.

You are going to build up the model that you are creating using the set of data for training. You can use the set of data for testing to verify the accuracy of the model's output. Doing these steps takes some time, but they are absolutely crucial to the process. If you don't do them, you could run into a big risk of overfitting the model. This means that you train the model with a set of data that is so limited that the model ends up picking out all of the characteristics, both the noise and the signal, that are only true for that set of data, rather than for all of the examples you want.

If you have a model that has overfitted for a specific set of data, it is going to end up performing horribly when you want to run it on some of the other sets of data that come in later, or that you are already storing. A test set of data ensures that the model is performing the way that you want and that you are getting the amount of accuracy that you need in the model.

4. Building the Model

Then we need to move on to the idea of building up our model. Sometimes the business objectives or the data that you have will lend themselves to a specific model or algorithm that you are able to use. If this is the case for you, go ahead and use that algorithm and see how the model can work. This saves you time and can make the predictive analysis so much easier to work with overall.

Then there are times when the best approach that you should use, even with the given data that you have - or the business objective in place - is not going to be as easy to figure out. This doesn't mean that you give up, though. It simply means that you need to do some research and figure out which method is going to be the best for you. And you may have to try out a few options a bit and see what kinds of predictions you are able to make with them.

As you take the time to explore the data that you have, don't be afraid to run as many different algorithms on it as you can. This allows you to see what happens with each one, and you can compare the outputs that you get here. You can then base your choice of the final model on the results that you got overall from these algorithms when they were put to work. This may not be the case all of the time, but sometimes you will find that the results are going to be shown better when you run an ensemble of models at the same time on the data, and then you can choose the final model that you would like to use by comparing the outputs that you see.

5. Deploying the Model that You Want to Use

After you go through the last step of building up your own model, it is time to actually deploy this model in order to get all of the benefits that come out of it. This is a process that is going to require coordination with some other departments, depending on which model you chose to use, and the overall goal of doing this model.

Your goal here is to build a model that is deployable, whether it is just going to be used in one area of your company or in many different parts of the company. You also want to make sure that you have a good method of presenting your results to business stakeholders in a manner that they are able to understand, and you have to convince others so that they are more likely to adopt the model that you have presented.

Once the model is deployed, you will need to monitor its performance, and you can make new improvements to this model as is needed. It is hard to know whether the model is working the way that you want if no one is monitoring it at all. It is common for a model to decay over time; it is not going to work perfectly forever, so watching how it does and updating it any time that you need by refreshing it with some new data as it becomes available can ensure that your model will continue to work the way that you want.

If you can follow these steps, and spend some time working with the different algorithms that are available, you will find that this is one of the best ways to put the predictive analysis to work for you. The steps are easy to work with; they just take some time as you gather up the data that you want, clean it and then make sure that you pick out the algorithm that works for your needs.

Even with the right algorithm, you need to make sure that you do training and testing along the way. It is never a good idea to just go with an algorithm and assume it is working and giving out accurate results. This is not worth your time and can lead you to make bad predictions and decisions. Instead, you need to focus on training, then testing the model, and double-checking that things match up the way that you want. And when this happens, you know that you have a predictive model that is going to work for your needs, and that will help you to make good predictions for your company, predictions that are going to be based on facts and data.

Conclusion

Thank you for making it through to the end of *Predictive Analysis*. Let's hope it was informative and able to provide you with all the tools you need to achieve your goals whatever they may be!

The next step is to start learning the best way that you can create your own predictive analysis for your company. You have already been collecting all of that data for some time now, why not learn what is inside all of that data, and how you can use that to provide better customer service, get your customers to feel better, to beat out the competition, and to pick out new products and services to offer on the market?

This guidebook took some time to explore the idea of predictive analysis, and all that it can do for you. There are a lot of options in regards to how to go about accomplishing this process, but you will find that with predictive analysis, you can be sure that you are approaching the information with the goal of making a prediction when it is all done.

We looked at the many different parts of predictive analysis, including working with data mining, machine learning, statistics, and so much more. All of these can be brought in at one point or another to make it easier to gather the data that you need, to clean it up so that it works with your chosen algorithm, and to ensure that you will actually glean some good information out of the process.

We also spent some time looking at the tips and tricks that you can follow in order to get the most out of any kind of predictive analysis that you do. This process is definitely worth your time, and it is going to help you get so much done and beat out the competition. You want to make sure that you are using the process in the right manner, to ensure you get the best results. The tips and suggestions that we provide in this guidebook will make sure that this happens for you.

When you are ready to work on your own predictive analysis, and you want to finally take all of that information you have been gathering and storing and put it to good use, make sure to check out this guidebook to see exactly how you can work on your own predictive analysis today.

Finally, if you found this book useful in any way, a review on Amazon is always appreciated!

Here are other books by Richard Hurley

BIG DATA

A Guide to Big Data Trends, Artificial Intelligence,
Machine Learning, Predictive Analytics,
Internet of Things, Data Science, Data Analytics,
Business Intelligence, and Data Mining

RICHARD HURLEY

Printed in Great Britain
by Amazon

86540407R00058